BEETLE

LIVING THINGS

BEETLE

Rebecca Stefoff

BENCHMARK BOOKS

MARSHALL CAVENDISH
NEW YORK

Benchmark Books
Marshall Cavendish Corporation
99 White Plains Road
Tarrytown, New York 10591-9001

Illustrations by Jean Cassels

Library of Congress Cataloging-in-Publication Data
Stefoff, Rebecca date
Beetle / Rebecca Stefoff.
p.   cm. — (Living things)
Includes bibliographical references and index.
Summary: Describes the physical characteristics, behavior, and
habitats of different kinds of beetles.
ISBN 0-7614-0410-4 (lib. bdg.)
1. Beetles—Juvenile literature. [1. Beetles.] I. Title.
II. Series: Stefoff, Rebecca Living things.
QL576.2.S74 1997 595.76—dc21   96-37592 CIP AC

Photo research by Ellen Barrett Dudley

Cover photo: *The National Audubon Collection/Photo Researchers, Inc.*,
J.H. Robinson

The photographs in this book are used by permission and through the courtesy of:
Peter Arnold, Inc.: Keith Kent, 2; C. Allen Morgan, 7; Hans Pfletschinger, 10, 11
(right), 12, 13 (top left & right, bottom left & right), 16, 17, 26; R.M. Meadows,
18 (right). *The National Audubon Collection/Photo Researchers, Inc.*: Joe
DiStefano, 6; Kjell B. Sandved, 8 (right), 9 (top & bottom), 18 (left), 20 (top &
bottom); Robert Noonan, 14–15; Scott Camazine, 21; Gary Retherford, 22, 25;
Dr. Paul A. Zahl, 24 (top); Stephen Dalton, 32. *Animals Animals*: Richard K. LaVal,
8 (right), G.I. Bernard/Oxford Scientific Films, 11 (left), Colin Milkins/Oxford
Scientific Films, 19; Michael Fogden, 23; Kjell Sandved/Oxford Scientific Films,
24 (bottom); Leen Van Der Slik, 27.

Printed in the United States of America

3   5   6   4   2

For Hannah

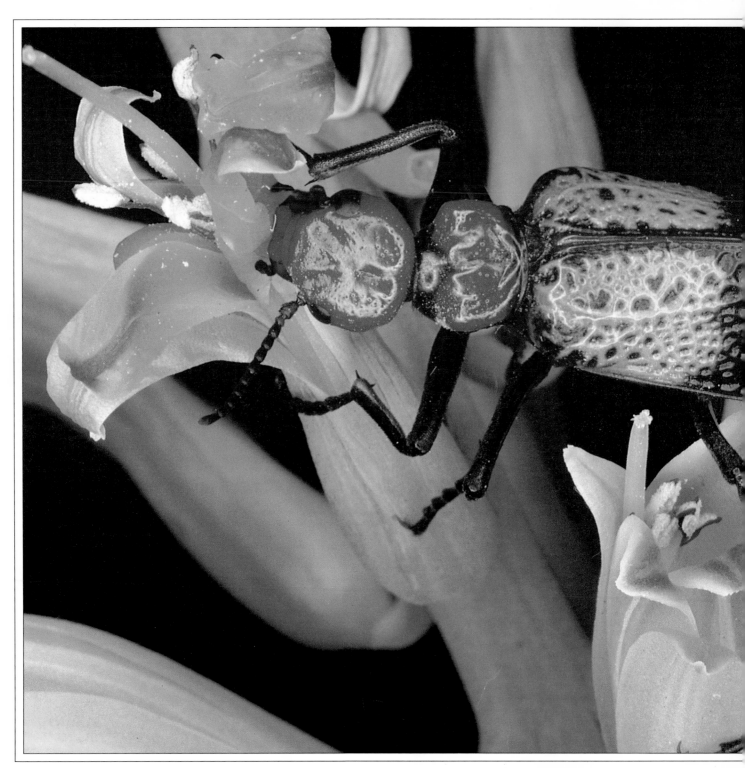

blister beetle eating aloe flower

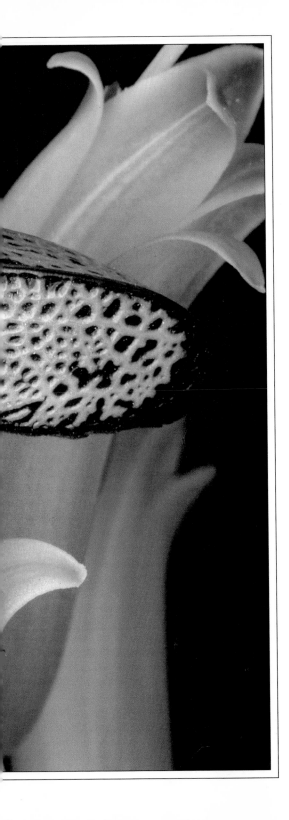

cypress or glorious beetle

The world is full of beetles. In forests and in fields, in gardens and in vacant lots, billions and billions of them are quietly going about their beetle business right now.

7

harlequin beetle, Costa Rica

leaf beetle, Mexico

All beetles belong to the insect family. These insects come in many shapes and sizes.

Some beetles are long and skinny, with long, skinny legs. Other beetles are short and round, with tiny little legs hidden under their shells.

metallic wood borer, Madagascar

Many beetles are flat and close to the ground. But other beetles have spines that stick up into the air. You don't ever want to step on a beetle—especially not a spiny one.

tortoise beetle, Bolivia

long-horned beetle

See the sharp hooks on the big beetle's mouth? This beetle eats insects. If the beetle's dinner runs away, the beetle catches it with those handy hooks.

Beetles have two sets of wings. The top wings are stiff. They are the beetle's suit of armor. When the beetle wants to fly, it opens the hard top wings and flies with the soft wings inside.

Even with four wings, some beetles never fly. They creep or run along the ground, smelling the air with their long, waving feelers.

Mother and father beetles come together to mate. Then the mother lays rows of little eggs.

Each egg hatches into a larva. The larva is like a plump worm. You might call it a caterpillar or a grub.

The larva eats as much as it can, and then it hangs very still and goes to sleep. Slowly it turns into a hard shell called a pupa. One day the pupa cracks open. Out crawls a grown-up beetle. Soon it will be ready to have eggs of its own.

female laying eggs　　　　　　　　　　*larva*

larva turning into pupa　　　　　　　　*adult beetle emerging from pupa*

Do you see all four stages of the Mexican bean beetle's life on this leaf?

First look for the eggs. Now look for the smallest larva. Can you find a larva that has started to get round and shiny? It is turning into a pupa.

The grown-up beetles are munching on the leaf. Look how many holes they have made. If these beetles eat much more, there won't be enough leaf left for them to stand on.

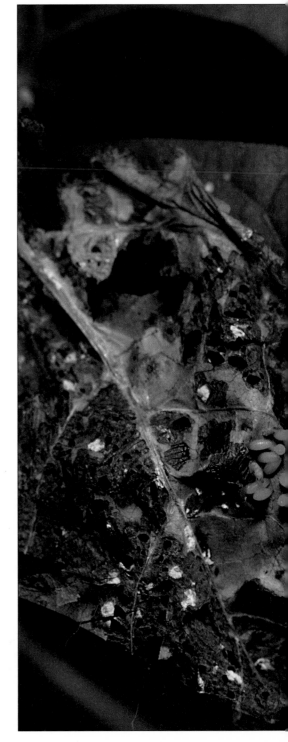

life cycle of Mexican bean beetle

Hunting beetles are the tigers of the forest floor. They eat other beetles and spiders, ants, worms, or snails. Hunting beetles run fast and pounce on the bugs and animals they eat.

beetle eating snail

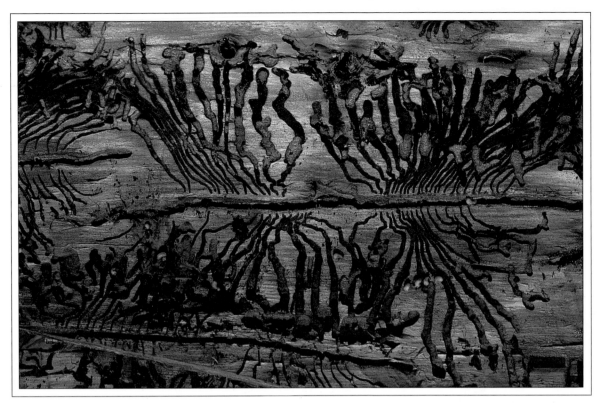

trails left by wood-boring beetles

Other beetles crawl along very slowly under the
bark of trees. They leave trails behind where they
have chewed the wood.

Can you spot the white beetle grubs in this tree?
Their mother laid her eggs in holes in the wood. As
soon as the grubs hatch, they can start nibbling on
the tasty wood.

snout beetle, South Africa *diving beetle with air bubble*

Beetles live just about everywhere.

Beetles who live in the driest deserts have hairs that hold tiny drops of dew. When the beetle needs a drink of water, it picks a drop off its back.

Other beetles swim underwater. They carry bubbles of air under their wings. When the beetle needs air, its legs move the bubble along its body. The beetle breathes the air through tiny holes in its sides.

Diving beetles don't like to walk on land. They spend most of their time underwater, hunting for water bugs and minnows. When they're tired of one pool or lake, they fly to another.

great diving beetle

giraffe beetles, Madagascar

There are more different kinds of beetles in the world than any other insect or animal. They look so different that it's hard to believe they're all beetles.

Take a look at the two red-and-black beetles with the long necks. They're called giraffe beetles. If you've ever seen a giraffe in a picture book or a zoo, you can guess why.

The smallest beetles in the world are fungus beetles, like the little red beetles on this page. And the smallest of all fungus beetles are smaller than the dot after this word.

fungus beetles, Panama

Hercules beetle, Costa Rica

One of the biggest beetles in the world is the
Hercules beetle. It lives in tropical rain forests. If you
put a big Hercules beetle on this page, it would reach
from the bottom of the page all the way to the top.

Hercules beetles sometimes fight with their long horns, trying to flip each other over. They don't hurt each other, though. The loser just runs away.

Hercules beetles, Costa Rica

diamond beetle, Philippines

Some beetles are shiny or sparkly. They look like pieces of jewelry flying or crawling around the forest.

You will probably never see a beetle like the silver-colored one on this page. The silver beetle is one of the rarest beetles in the world. It lives in tropical rain forests, along with the Hercules beetle.

silver beetle, Costa Rica

ladybug

You don't have to go to the rain forest to see beetles.

Have you ever seen a ladybug? Maybe you call it a ladybird. Ladybugs live all over North America.

The next time you see a ladybug you can say, "Hey, there's a beetle! It's part of the biggest family on earth."

blister beetles, South Africa

A QUICK LOOK AT THE BEETLE

Beetles are insects, like ants and flies. What makes beetles special is their set of stiff front wings that form a hard shell over their backs. Only beetles have these heavy wings that are not used for flying.

There are about three hundred thousand kinds of beetles. Every year scientists find two or three thousand new kinds. Some experts think that there may be a million more kinds of beetles waiting to be discovered.

Here are six kinds of beetles along with their scientific names in Latin and a few facts.

GOLDEN TORTOISE BEETLE
Metriona bicolor   (mee tree OH nah BEE coh lohr)
Lives throughout the United States. Round, turtle-shaped body is about half an inch long (1.2 cm). Shiny gold while alive, but dull yellowish-gray when dead.

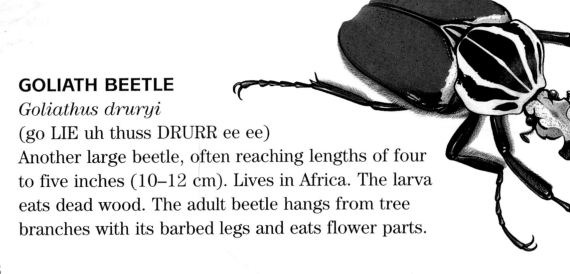

GOLIATH BEETLE
Goliathus druryi
(go LIE uh thuss DRURR ee ee)
Another large beetle, often reaching lengths of four to five inches (10–12 cm). Lives in Africa. The larva eats dead wood. The adult beetle hangs from tree branches with its barbed legs and eats flower parts.

TIGER BEETLE
Megacephala carolina
(meh gah SEFF ah la care oh LEE nah)
Slender beetle with long antennae (feelers). Usually less than
an inch long (2.5 cm). Back is iridescent blue, purple, and green. Eats other
insects. Runs and flies quickly, jumps on its prey. Likes open sandy areas.
Lives in southeastern United States.

ROUND-NECKED LONG-HORNED BEETLE
Rosalia funebris
(roe ZAY lee ah fyoo NEB riss)
Belongs to "long-horned" group of beetles,
named not for horns but for their long antennae.
Usually about an inch in length, with white and
chocolate-brown markings. The larva eats wood.
Adults eat flower parts.

GIANT STAG BEETLE
Lucanus elaphus
(loo CAY nus ELL uh fuss)
Largest stag beetle in the United States, measuring
up to 2.5 inches (6.4 cm). Its branching horns look
like a stag's antlers. Lives from Virginia and North
Carolina in the east to Oklahoma in the west.

HERCULES BEETLE

Dynastes herculeanus
(dy NASS tees her kew LAY nus)
One of world's largest beetles. Can reach a
length of seven to eight inches (18–20 cm),
including horn. Lives in Central and
South America.

Taking Care of the Beetle

Some beetles and their larvae are harmful to people. They destroy timber
and crops. But beetles also do a lot of good. Beetles are part of the web of
life in soil, trees, and grasslands. They clean up dead plants and animals by
eating them, and they eat other insects that could become pests. We need
to protect fields, forests, and other wild places so that beetles will always
be part of our world.

Find Out More

Johnson, Sylvia A. *Beetles*. Minneapolis: Lerner Publications, 1982.

Milne, Lorus J. *Nature's Clean-Up Crew: The Burying Beetles*. New York: Dodd, Mead, 1982.

Patent, Dorothy H. *Beetles and How They Live*. New York: Holiday House, 1978.

Penny, Malcolm. *Discovering Beetles*. New York: Bookwright Press, 1986.

Still, John. *Amazing Beetles*. New York: Knopf, 1991.

Watts, Barrie. *Beetles*. New York: Franklin Watts, 1989.

Index

Rebecca Stefoff has published many books for young readers. Science and environmental issues are among her favorite subjects. She lives in Oregon and enjoys observing the natural world while hiking, camping, and scuba diving.

cockchafer beetle